13
1·50

CUPCAKES

Contents

Welcome!

Not only am I a dedicated and enthusiastic cook, but I love nothing more than encouraging those who think they are domestically challenged to pick up a pan and a spoon and get stirring. It doesn't take much to grasp the basics and from there, anything is possible. Hiding behind the mantra 'I can't cook' only brings fear into the kitchen, but it is these mistakes that will ultimately make you a better, more confident and knowledgeable cook. All it takes is some good recipes and plenty of enthusiasm and kitchen domination will surely follow. Luckily, all Good Housekeeping cookery books are filled with tempting recipes with clear methods and realistic photography – we are taking the chance out of cooking as our recipes are guaranteed to work.

If you have ever tried turning the page of a cookery book with dirty hands, while also balancing a steaming pan and a sticky spoon, then you will love the flip-chart design of this book. The simple fact that the recipes stand upright makes for an easier cooking experience – say goodbye to hovering over recipes while trying to stop the spoon dripping on to the pages.

This Good Housekeeping Flip It! book collection is filled with meticulously triple-tested recipes that have been developed and put through their paces in our dedicated test kitchens. We hope you enjoy the recipes and that they inspire you to give them a try – you know that they'll work after all!

Meike.

Meike Beck
Cookery Editor

Peanut Butter Cupcakes

Makes 12

Preparation Time
30 minutes

Cooking Time
25 minutes,
plus cooling
and setting

Per Cupcake
363 calories
17g fat
(of which 7g saturates)
49g carbohydrate
0.5g salt

75g (3oz) unsalted peanuts or cashew nuts, toasted
100g (3½oz) unsalted butter, softened
50g (2oz) light soft brown sugar
50g (2oz) dark muscovado sugar
3 medium eggs
175g (6oz) self-raising flour, sifted
½ tsp baking powder

For the topping and decoration
100ml (3½fl oz) milk
50g (2oz) cocoa powder
300g (11oz) icing sugar
100g (3½oz) peanut butter
chocolate sprinkles or vermicelli

1 Preheat the oven to 190°C (170°C fan oven) mark 5. Line a 12-hole muffin tin with paper muffin cases.

2 Whiz the peanuts or cashews in a food processor until finely ground. Set aside.

3 Using a hand-held electric whisk, whisk the butter with the light brown and muscovado sugars, or beat with a wooden spoon, until pale and creamy. Gradually whisk in the eggs until just combined. Using a metal spoon, fold in the flour, baking powder and finely ground nuts until combined. Divide the mixture equally between the paper cases.

4 Bake for 20 minutes or until golden and risen. Leave to cool in the tin for 5 minutes, then transfer to a wire rack to cool completely.

5 For the topping, warm the milk in a small saucepan. Sift the cocoa and icing sugar into a large bowl, then gradually stir in the warm milk until it forms a smooth icing.

6 Put a small spoonful of peanut butter on the top of each cake and then spoon the chocolate icing on to cover the peanut butter and to coat the top of the cupcake. Decorate with sprinkles or vermicelli. Stand the cakes upright on the wire rack and leave for about 1 hour to set.

Breakfast Cupcakes

Makes 12

Preparation Time
30 minutes

Cooking Time
20 minutes,
plus cooling
and setting

Per Cupcake
327 calories
14g fat
(of which 8g saturates)
48g carbohydrate
0.3g salt

175g (6oz) unsalted butter, softened
100g (3½oz) caster sugar
3 medium eggs
75g (3oz) apricot jam
150g (5oz) self-raising flour, sifted
75g (3oz) oatbran
½ tsp baking powder

For the icing and decoration
225g (8oz) icing sugar
1–2 tbsp orange juice
75g (3oz) mixed berry granola

1 Preheat the oven to 190°C (170°C fan oven) mark 5. Line a 12-hole muffin tin with paper muffin cases.

2 Using a hand-held electric whisk, whisk the butter and caster sugar in a bowl, or beat with a wooden spoon, until pale and creamy. Gradually whisk in the eggs until just combined. Using a metal spoon, fold in the apricot jam, flour, oatbran and baking powder until combined. Divide the mixture equally between the paper cases.

3 Bake for 20 minutes or until golden and risen. Leave to cool in the tin for 5 minutes, then transfer to a wire rack to cool completely.

4 For the icing, sift the icing sugar into a bowl, then add enough orange juice to achieve a smooth, thick icing. Spoon a little on top of each cake, then sprinkle with the granola. Stand the cakes upright on the wire rack and leave for about 1 hour to set.

Toast & Marmalade Cupcakes

Makes 12
Preparation Time
30 minutes
Cooking Time
20–25 minutes,
plus cooling
and setting

Per Cupcake
336 calories
10g fat
(of which 2g saturates)
57g carbohydrate
1.5g salt

150g (5oz) low-fat olive oil spread
200g (7oz) wholemeal self-raising
flour, sifted
150g (5oz) light soft brown sugar
3 medium eggs
50g (2oz) marmalade
100ml (3½fl oz) milk
zest of 1 orange
50g (2oz) fresh wholemeal
breadcrumbs

For the icing and decoration
125g (4oz) marmalade
300g (11oz) icing sugar, sifted

1 Preheat the oven to 180°C (160°C fan oven) mark 4. Line a 12-hole muffin tin with paper muffin cases.

2 Put the low-fat spread, flour, brown sugar, eggs, marmalade, milk, orange zest and breadcrumbs into a large bowl. Using a hand-held electric whisk, whisk together until pale and creamy. Divide the mixture equally between the paper cases.

3 Bake for 20–25 minutes until golden and risen. Leave to cool in the tin for 5 minutes, then transfer to a wire rack to cool completely.

4 For the icing, pass the marmalade through a sieve into a bowl to remove the rind. Reserve the rind. Mix the icing sugar with the sieved marmalade in a bowl until it forms a smooth icing. Spoon a little icing on to each cake to flood the top, then scatter on the reserved rind. Stand the cakes upright on the wire rack and leave for about 1 hour to set.

Mini Green Tea Cupcakes

Makes 12
Preparation Time
40 minutes
Cooking Time
25 minutes, plus
cooling and
infusing

Per Cupcake
282 calories
13g fat
(of which 8g saturates)
41g carbohydrate
0.3g salt

100ml (3½fl oz) milk
2 tsp loose green tea leaves
100g (3½oz) unsalted butter, softened
125g (4oz) caster sugar
2 medium eggs
150g (5oz) self-raising flour, sifted
¼ tsp baking powder

For the topping and decoration
3 tsp loose green tea leaves
75g (3oz) unsalted butter, softened
250g (9oz) icing sugar, sifted
ready-made sugar flowers

1 Preheat the oven to 190°C (170°C fan oven) mark 5. Line a 12-hole muffin tin with paper fairy cake or bun cases.

2 Put the milk into a small saucepan and bring to the boil. Add the green tea leaves and leave to infuse for 30 minutes.

3 Using a hand-held electric whisk, whisk the butter and caster sugar in a bowl, or beat with a wooden spoon, until pale and creamy. Gradually whisk in the eggs until just combined. Pass the green tea milk through a sieve into the bowl, then discard the tea. Using a metal spoon, fold in the flour and baking powder until combined. Divide the mixture equally between the paper cases.

4 Bake for 18–20 minutes until golden and risen. Leave to cool in the tin for 5 minutes, then transfer to a wire rack to cool completely.

5 For the topping, put the green tea leaves into a jug, add about 75ml (2½fl oz) boiling water and leave to infuse for 5 minutes. Put the butter into a bowl and whisk until fluffy. Gradually add the icing sugar and whisk until combined. Pass the green tea through a sieve into the bowl, then discard the tea. Continue to whisk until light and fluffy.

6 Insert a star nozzle into a piping bag, then fill the bag with the buttercream and pipe a swirl on to the top of each cake. Decorate each with a sugar flower.

Lavender & Honey Cupcakes

Makes 9
Preparation Time
35 minutes
Cooking Time
15–20 minutes,
plus cooling and
setting

Per Cupcake
316 calories
13g fat
(of which 8g saturates)
50g carbohydrate
0.3g salt

125g (4oz) unsalted butter, softened
125g (4oz) runny honey
2 medium eggs
125g (4oz) self-raising flour, sifted
1 tsp baking powder

For the icing and decoration
3 honey and lavender tea bags
2 tsp unsalted butter
250g (9oz) icing sugar, sifted
red and blue food colouring
purple sugar stars
edible silver dust (optional)

1 Preheat the oven to 190°C (170°C fan oven) mark 5. Line a 12-hole muffin tin with 9 paper muffin cases.

2 Using a hand-held electric whisk, whisk the butter and honey in a bowl, or beat with a wooden spoon, until combined. Gradually whisk in the eggs until just combined. Using a metal spoon, fold in the flour and baking powder until combined. Divide the mixture equally between the paper cases.

3 Bake for 15–20 minutes until golden and risen. Leave to cool in the tin for 5 minutes, then transfer to a wire rack to cool completely.

4 For the icing, infuse the tea bags in 50ml (2fl oz) boiling water in a small bowl for 5 minutes. Remove the tea bags and squeeze out the excess water into the bowl. Stir in the butter until melted. Put the icing sugar into a large bowl, add the infused tea mixture and stir to make a smooth icing. Add a few drops of blue and red food colouring until it is lilac in colour.

5 Spoon a little icing on top of each cake, to flood the tops, then sprinkle with stars. Stand the cakes upright on the wire rack and leave for about 1 hour to set. Dust with edible dust, if you like, when set.

Sticky Gingerbread Cupcakes

Makes 9
Preparation Time
35 minutes
Cooking Time
20 minutes,
plus cooling

Per Cupcake
386 calories
17g fat
(of which 11g saturates)
58g carbohydrate
0.5g salt

175g (6oz) self-raising flour
75g (3oz) unsalted butter, chilled and cut into cubes
¼ tsp bicarbonate of soda
2 tsp ground ginger
25g (1oz) stem ginger in syrup, finely chopped,
plus 3 tbsp syrup from the jar
50g (2oz) dark muscovado sugar
50g (2oz) golden syrup
50g (2oz) treacle
juice of 1 orange
2 medium eggs, beaten

For the topping and decoration
100g (3½oz) unsalted butter, softened
200g (7oz) icing sugar, sifted
3 tbsp syrup from the stem ginger jar
1 tsp ground ginger
ready-made sugar flowers (optional)

1 Preheat the oven to 190°C (170°C fan oven) mark 5. Line a 12-hole muffin tin with 9 paper muffin cases.

2 Put the flour into a large bowl and, using your fingertips, rub in the butter until it resembles breadcrumbs. Stir in the bicarbonate of soda, ground ginger and stem ginger and set aside. Put the muscovado sugar, syrup, treacle and orange juice into a small saucepan and heat gently until the sugar dissolves. Leave to cool for 5 minutes.

3 Mix the eggs and warm sugar mixture into the flour mixture and stir with a spatula until just combined. Divide equally between the paper cases.

4 Bake for 20 minutes or until golden and risen. Remove from the oven and drizzle each cake with 1 tsp ginger syrup. Leave to cool in the tin for 5 minutes, then transfer to a wire rack to cool completely.

5 For the buttercream topping, put the butter into a bowl and whisk until fluffy. Add the icing sugar, ginger syrup and ground ginger. Whisk until light and fluffy. Using a small palette knife, spread a little buttercream over the top of each cake. Decorate with sugar flowers, if you like.

Ginger & Lemon Cupcakes

Makes 12

Preparation Time
15 minutes

Cooking Time
20 minutes,
plus cooling

Per Cupcake
246 calories
10g fat
(of which 2g saturates)
40g carbohydrate
0.4g salt

125g (4oz) self-raising flour
125g (4oz) caster sugar
125g (4oz) soft margarine or butter
1 tsp baking powder
1 tsp ground ginger
grated zest of 1 unwaxed lemon
2 large eggs
50g (2oz) crystallised (candied) ginger, chopped, plus extra to decorate

For the icing and decoration
200g (7oz) icing sugar, sifted
juice of 1 lemon

1 Preheat the oven to 190°C (170°C fan oven) mark 5. Line a 12-hole muffin tin with paper muffin cases.

2 Sift the flour and sugar into a large bowl, food processor or mixer. Add the margarine, baking powder, ground ginger, lemon zest and eggs and beat well until pale and creamy. Gently fold in the chopped crystallised ginger.

3 Divide the mixture equally between the cases and bake for 20 minutes or until golden and firm to the touch. Transfer to a wire rack to cool completely.

4 For the icing, put the icing sugar into a bowl, then slowly add the lemon juice and mix well. If you need a little more liquid, add a few drops of boiling water. Spread the icing over and top with a little chunk of the extra crystallised ginger.

Honeycomb Cream Cupcakes

Makes 9
Preparation Time
30 minutes
Cooking Time
20 minutes,
plus cooling

Per Cupcake
480 calories
25g fat
(of which 15g saturates)
65g carbohydrate
0.6g salt

125g (4oz) unsalted butter, softened
50g (2oz) caster sugar
2 medium eggs
75g (3oz) runny honey
125g (4oz) self-raising flour, sifted
50g (2oz) rolled oats
½ tsp baking powder
1 tbsp milk

For the topping and decoration
125g (4oz) unsalted butter, softened
300g (11oz) golden icing sugar, sifted
2 tbsp milk
1 Crunchie bar, thinly sliced

1 Preheat the oven to 190°C (170°C fan oven) mark 5. Line a 12-hole muffin tin with 9 paper muffin cases.

2 Using a hand-held electric whisk, whisk the butter and caster sugar in a bowl, or beat with a wooden spoon, until pale and creamy. Gradually whisk in the eggs and honey until just combined. Using a metal spoon, fold in the flour, oats, baking powder and milk until combined. Divide the mixture equally between the paper cases.

3 Bake for 20 minutes or until golden and risen. Leave to cool in the tin for 5 minutes, then transfer to a wire rack to cool completely.

4 For the topping, put the butter into a bowl and whisk until fluffy. Gradually whisk in half the icing sugar, then add the milk and the remaining icing sugar and whisk until light and fluffy.

5 Insert a star nozzle into a piping bag, then fill the bag with the buttercream and pipe a swirl on to the top of each cake. When ready to serve, decorate each with a few slices of Crunchie.

Pistachio & Polenta Cupcakes

Makes 12

Preparation Time
35 minutes

Cooking Time
25 minutes,
plus cooling

Per Cupcake
542 calories
33g fat
(of which 13g saturates)
56g carbohydrate
0.6g salt

150g (5oz) shelled pistachio nuts
175g (6oz) unsalted butter, softened
175g (6oz) caster sugar
3 medium eggs
200g (7oz) fine polenta
½ tsp baking powder
150g (5oz) ground almonds
zest of 2 lemons
2 tbsp milk

For the icing
75g (3oz) unsalted butter, softened
300g (11oz) icing sugar, sifted
juice of 2 lemons

1 Preheat the oven to 180°C (160°C fan oven) mark 4. Line a 12-hole muffin tin with paper muffin cases.

2 Whiz the pistachios in a food processor until really finely chopped.

3 Using a hand-held electric whisk, whisk the butter and caster sugar in a bowl, or beat with a wooden spoon, until pale and creamy. Gradually whisk in the eggs until just combined. Using a metal spoon, fold in the polenta, baking powder, ground almonds, lemon zest, milk and 100g (3½oz) ground pistachios until combined. Divide the mixture equally between the paper cases.

4 Bake for 25 minutes or until golden and risen. Leave to cool in the tin for 5 minutes, then transfer to a wire rack to cool completely.

5 For the icing, put the butter into a bowl and whisk until fluffy. Gradually whisk in half the icing sugar, then add the lemon juice and the remaining icing sugar, whisking until light and fluffy. Using a small palette knife, spread a little of the buttercream over the top of each cake, then sprinkle with a little of the remaining chopped pistachios.

Gluten free

Aniseed Cupcakes

Makes 12
Preparation Time
30 minutes
Cooking Time
20–25 minutes,
plus cooling

Per Cupcake
291 calories
15g fat
(of which 9g saturates)
37g carbohydrate
0.4g salt

125g (4oz) unsalted butter, softened
200g (7oz) caster sugar
2 medium eggs
200g (7oz) self-raising flour, sifted
25g (1oz) custard powder
2 tbsp caraway seeds
125ml (4fl oz) milk

For the topping and decoration
75g (3oz) unsalted butter, softened
300g (11oz) icing sugar, sifted
2 tbsp Pernod
pale blue sugar sprinkles

1 Preheat the oven to 190°C (170°C fan oven) mark 5. Line a 12-hole muffin tin with paper muffin cases.

2 Using a hand-held electric whisk, whisk the butter and caster sugar in a bowl, or beat with a wooden spoon, until pale and creamy. Gradually whisk in the eggs until just combined. Using a metal spoon, fold in the flour, custard powder, caraway seeds and milk until combined. Divide the mixture equally between the paper cases.

3 Bake for 20–25 minutes until golden and risen. Leave to cool in the tin for 5 minutes, then transfer to a wire rack to cool completely.

4 For the topping, put the butter into a bowl and whisk until fluffy. Gradually whisk in half the icing sugar, then add the Pernod, 1 tbsp boiling water and the remaining icing sugar and whisk until light and fluffy. Using a small palette knife, spread a little of the buttercream over the top of each cake, then sprinkle with the blue sugar sprinkles.

Nutty Cupcakes

Makes 12

Preparation Time
40 minutes

Cooking Time
25 minutes,
plus cooling
and setting

Per Cupcake
338 calories
23g fat
(of which 10g saturates)
31g carbohydrate
0.4g salt

150g (5oz) unsalted butter, softened
175g (6oz) self-raising flour, sifted
50g (2oz) caster sugar
100ml (3½fl oz) golden syrup
3 medium eggs
1 tsp baking powder
1 tsp ground mixed spice
50g (2oz) mixed chopped nuts

For the topping
3 tbsp double cream
1 tbsp milk
50g (2oz) milk chocolate, finely chopped
25g (1oz) dark chocolate, finely chopped
75g (3oz) roasted chopped hazelnuts

1 Preheat the oven to 190°C (170°C fan oven) mark 5. Line a 12-hole muffin tin with paper muffin cases.

2 Put the butter, flour, sugar, syrup, eggs, baking powder, mixed spice and nuts into a large bowl. Using a hand-held electric whisk, whisk together until pale and creamy. Divide the mixture equally between the paper cases.

3 Bake for 20 minutes or until golden and risen. Leave to cool in the tin for 5 minutes, then transfer to a wire rack to cool completely.

4 For the topping, heat the cream and milk in a small saucepan until nearly boiling. Put both chocolates into a bowl and pour the hot cream over them. Leave to stand for 5 minutes, then gently stir until smooth.

5 Put the hazelnuts into a shallow bowl. Dip the top of each cake into the chocolate cream, allow the excess to drip off, then dip into the hazelnuts until coated all over. Stand the cakes upright on the wire rack and leave for about 1 hour to set.

Dainty Cupcakes

Makes 12
Preparation Time
15 minutes,
plus drying
Cooking Time
15–20 minutes,
plus cooling
and setting

Per Cupcake
306 calories
14g fat
(of which 8g saturates)
46g carbohydrate
0.4g salt

175g (6oz) unsalted butter, softened
175g (6oz) golden caster sugar
3 medium eggs
175g (6oz) self-raising flour, sifted
finely grated zest and juice of 1 lemon

For the frosted flowers
1 medium egg white
6 edible flowers, such as violas
caster sugar to dust

For the icing
225g (8oz) icing sugar, sifted
1 drop violet food colouring
2–3 tbsp lemon juice, strained

1 Preheat the oven to 190°C (170°C fan oven) mark 5. Line a 12-hole bun tin or muffin tin with paper muffin cases.

2 Put the butter and caster sugar into a bowl and cream together until pale, light and fluffy. Add the eggs, one at a time, and beat together, folding 1 tbsp flour into the mixture if it looks as if it is going to curdle. Fold in the flour, lemon zest and juice and mix well.

3 Spoon the mixture into the paper cases and bake for 15–20 minutes until pale golden, risen and springy to the touch. Transfer to a wire rack to cool completely.

4 To make the frosted flowers, whisk the egg white in a clean bowl for 30 seconds or until frothy. Brush over the flower petals and put on a wire rack resting on a piece of greaseproof paper. Dust heavily with caster sugar, then leave the flowers to dry.

5 To make the icing, put the icing sugar into a bowl with the food colouring. Mix in the lemon juice to make a smooth dropping consistency. Spoon the icing on to the cakes, then decorate with the frosted flowers. Stand the cakes upright on the wire rack and leave for about 1 hour to set.

Vanilla Cupcakes

Makes 12

Preparation Time
15 minutes

Cooking Time
20 minutes,
plus cooling
and setting

125g (4oz) unsalted butter, softened
125g (4oz) golden caster sugar
2 medium eggs
125g (4oz) self-raising flour
1 tbsp vanilla extract

For the topping
200g (7oz) white chocolate, broken
into pieces

1 Preheat the oven to 190°C (170°C fan oven) mark 5.
Line a 12-hole bun tin or muffin pan with paper cases.

2 Put the butter, sugar, eggs, flour and vanilla into
a large bowl and beat thoroughly until smooth and
creamy. Half-fill the paper cases with the mixture and bake
for 15–20 minutes or until pale golden, risen and springy
to the touch. Transfer to a wire rack to cool completely.

3 For the topping, melt the chocolate in a heatproof
bowl set over a pan of gently simmering water,
making sure the base of the bowl doesn't touch the water.
Stir until smooth, then leave to cool slightly. Spoon the
chocolate over the cakes and leave for about 1 hour to set.

Vanilla & White Chocolate Cupcakes

Makes 12
Preparation Time
25 minutes
Cooking Time
15–20 minutes,
plus cooling
and setting

Per Cupcake
270 calories
15g fat
(of which 9g saturates)
32g carbohydrate
0.2g salt

125g (4oz) unsalted butter, at room
temperature
125g (4oz) golden caster sugar
1 vanilla pod
2 medium eggs
125g (4oz) self-raising flour, sifted
1 tbsp vanilla extract

For the topping and decoration
200g (7oz) white chocolate, broken
into pieces
12 crystallised violets or frosted flowers
(see Cook's Tip)

1 Preheat the oven to 190°C (170°C fan oven) mark 5.
Line a 12-hole bun tin or muffin tin with paper
muffin cases.

2 Put the butter and sugar into a bowl. Split the vanilla
pod lengthways, scrape out the seeds and add to the
bowl. Add the eggs, flour and vanilla and then, using a
hand-held electric whisk, beat thoroughly until smooth
and creamy. Spoon the mixture into the paper cases.

3 Bake for 15–20 minutes until pale golden, risen and
springy to the touch. Leave in the tin for 2–3 minutes,
then transfer to a wire rack to cool completely.

4 For the topping, melt the chocolate in a heatproof
bowl set over a pan of gently simmering water,
making sure the base of the bowl doesn't touch the water.
Stir until smooth and leave to cool slightly. Spoon the
chocolate on to the cakes and top with a frosted flower.
Stand the cakes upright on the wire rack and leave for
about 1 hour to set.

Cook's Tip
To make the frosted flowers, whisk 1 medium egg white
in a clean bowl for 30 seconds or until frothy. Brush it
over 12 violet petals and put on a wire rack. Lightly dust
with caster sugar and leave to dry.

Lemon & Vanilla Cupcakes

Makes 12
Preparation Time
25 minutes
Cooking Time
15 minutes,
plus cooling

Per Cupcake
387 calories
21g fat
(of which 13g saturates)
47g carbohydrate
0.6 salt

200g (7oz) golden caster sugar
200g (7oz) unsalted butter, very soft
finely grated zest and juice of one lemon
4 medium eggs, beaten
200g (7oz) self-raising flower

For the icing and decoration
75g (3oz) unsalted butter, softened
175g (6oz) icing sugar, sifted
1–2 tbsp milk
1 tsp vanilla extract
Selection of sugar sprinkles

1 Preheat the oven to 200°C (180°C fan oven) mark 6. Line a 12-hole muffin tin with paper muffin cases.

2 Put the sugar, butter and lemon zest into a large bowl, and using a hand-held electric whisk, whisk together until pale and creamy. Beat in the eggs a little at a time, folding in 1 tbsp flour if the mixture looks as if it is about to curdle.

3 Using a metal spoon, fold in the flour and lemon juice. Divide the mixture equally between the paper cases. Bake for 12–15 minutes until golden. Transfer to a wire rack to cool.

4 For the icing, put the butter into a large bowl and beat in two-thirds of the icing sugar with a hand-held electric whisk. Gradually beat in the rest of the icing sugar with the milk and vanilla until you have a soft but spreadable consistency that holds its shape.

5 When the cakes are completely cold, top each one with icing and swirl with a flat-bladed knife to form peaks. Decorate with sugar sprinkles.

Citrus Cupcakes

Makes 12
Preparation Time
15 minutes
Cooking Time
20 minutes,
plus cooling

Per Cupcake
362 calories
21g fat
(of which 8g saturates)
42g carbohydrate
0.4g salt

125g (4oz) self-raising flour
1 tsp baking powder
125g (4oz) caster sugar
125g (4oz) soft margarine or butter
2 large eggs
grated zest of 2 large unwaxed lemons,
plus extra shreds, to decorate (optional)
1 tbsp freshly squeezed lemon juice

For the topping
1 × 125g (4oz) jar lemon curd
200ml (7fl oz) crème fraîche

1 Preheat the oven to 190°C (170°C fan oven) mark 5. Line a 12-hole muffin tin with paper muffin cases.

2 Sift the flour, baking powder and sugar into a large bowl, food processor or mixer. Add the margarine, eggs, lemon zest and juice and beat until light and fluffy.

3 Spoon the mixture into the cases and bake for about 20 minutes until firm to the touch and golden. Transfer to a wire rack to cool completely.

4 For the topping, use a small, sharp knife to slice the top off each cake, then place a generous spoonful of lemon curd on top of the cake and put the lid back on.

5 Add a dollop of crème fraîche and a few tiny shreds of lemon zest, if you like.

Tropical Burst Cupcakes

Makes 12

Preparation Time
35 minutes

Cooking Time
20 minutes,
plus cooling
and setting

Per Cupcake
256 calories
8g fat
(of which 1g saturates)
45g carbohydrate
0.2g salt

200g (7oz) self-raising flour, sifted
½ tsp bicarbonate of soda
100g (3½oz) caster sugar
50g (2oz) ready-to-eat dried
tropical fruit, finely chopped
3 medium eggs
100ml (3½fl oz) sunflower oil
75ml (2½fl oz) buttermilk
1 × 227g tin pineapple pieces,
drained and finely chopped

For the topping and decoration
225g (8oz) royal icing sugar, sifted
zest and juice of 1 lime
sugar decorations (optional)

1 Preheat the oven to 190°C (170°C fan oven) mark 5. Line a 12-hole muffin tin with paper muffin cases.

2 Put the flour, bicarbonate of soda, caster sugar and dried fruit into a large bowl. Put the eggs, oil and buttermilk into a jug and lightly beat together until combined. Pour the oil mixture and the pineapple pieces into the flour and stir with a spatula until just combined. Divide the mixture equally between the paper cases.

3 Bake for 20 minutes or until lightly golden and risen. Leave to cool in the tin for 5 minutes, then transfer to a wire rack to cool completely.

4 For the topping, put the icing sugar, lime juice and zest and 1 tbsp cold water into a bowl and whisk for 5 minutes or until soft peaks form. Using a small palette knife, spread a little over the top of each cake. Stand the cakes upright on the wire rack, scatter with sugar decorations, if you like, and leave for about 1 hour to set.

Mango & Passion Fruit Cupcakes

Makes 12
Preparation Time
30 minutes
Cooking Time
25 minutes,
plus cooling

Per Cupcake
374 calories
18g fat
(of which 11g saturates)
52g carbohydrate
0.4g salt

4 ripe passion fruit
about 75ml (2½fl oz) orange juice
150g (5oz) unsalted butter, softened
250g (9oz) plain flour, sifted
175g (6oz) caster sugar
3 medium eggs
1 tbsp baking powder
75g (3oz) ready-to-eat dried mango,
finely chopped

For the topping and decoration
100g (3½oz) cream cheese
25g (1oz) unsalted butter, softened
200g (7oz) icing sugar, sifted
1 large, ripe passion fruit
white sugar sprinkles

1 Preheat the oven to 180°C (160°C fan oven) mark 4. Line a 12-hole muffin tin with paper muffin cases.

2 Cut the passion fruit in half and pass the seeds and juice through a sieve into a jug. Discard the seeds. You need 150ml (¼ pint) liquid, so use the orange juice to top up the passion fruit juice.

3 Put the butter, flour, caster sugar, eggs, baking powder and passion fruit and orange juice into a large bowl. Using a hand-held electric whisk, whisk together, or beat with a wooden spoon, until pale and creamy. Add the chopped mango and fold through until combined. Divide the mixture equally between the paper cases.

4 Bake for 25 minutes or until golden and risen. Leave to cool in the tin for 5 minutes, then transfer to a wire rack to cool completely.

5 For the topping, whisk together the cream cheese and butter until fluffy. Gradually add the icing sugar until combined. Cut the passion fruit in half and pass the seeds and juice through a sieve into the icing. Discard the seeds. Stir to combine, then, using a small palette knife, spread a little over the top of each cake. Scatter on the sugar sprinkles.

Cherry Bakewell Cupcakes

Makes 12
Preparation Time
30 minutes
Cooking Time
25 minutes,
plus cooling
and setting

Per Cupcake
405 calories
21g fat
(of which 11g saturates)
53g carbohydrate
0.4g salt

175g (6oz) unsalted butter, softened
175g (6oz) caster sugar
3 medium eggs
150g (5oz) self-raising flour, sifted
1 tsp baking powder
75g (3oz) ground almonds
1 tsp almond extract
75g (3oz) glacé cherries, finely
chopped

For the topping and decoration
1 tbsp custard powder
100ml (3½fl oz) milk
50g (2oz) unsalted butter, softened
250g (9oz) icing sugar, sifted
red sugar sprinkles

1 Preheat the oven to 190°C (170°C fan oven) mark 5.
Line a 12-hole muffin tin with paper muffin cases.

2 Using a hand-held electric whisk, whisk the butter
and caster sugar in a bowl, or beat with a wooden
spoon, until pale and creamy. Gradually whisk in the
eggs until just combined. Using a metal spoon, fold in
the flour, baking powder, ground almonds, almond
extract and cherries until combined. Divide the mixture
equally between the paper cases.

3 Bake for 20 minutes or until golden and risen. Leave
to cool in the tin for 5 minutes, then transfer to a wire
rack to cool completely.

4 For the topping, put the custard powder into a jug
and add a little of the milk to make a smooth paste.
Put the remaining milk into a saucepan and bring just
to the boil. Pour the hot milk on to the custard paste
and stir. Return to the milk pan and heat gently for
1–2 minutes until it thickens. Remove from the heat,
cover with dampened greaseproof paper to prevent a
skin forming and cool completely.

5 Put the custard into a bowl and, using an electric
whisk, whisk in the butter. Chill for 30 minutes.

6 Gradually whisk the icing sugar into the chilled
custard mixture until you have a smooth, thick icing.
Using a small palette knife, spread a little custard cream
over the top of each cake, then decorate with sugar
sprinkles. Stand the cakes upright on the wire rack and
leave for about 1 hour to set.

Pavlova Cupcakes

Makes 12

Preparation Time
30 minutes

Cooking Time
25 minutes,
plus cooling
and setting

Per Cupcake
226 calories
10g fat
(of which 6g saturates)
34g carbohydrate
0.2g salt

125g (4oz) unsalted butter, softened
100g (3½oz) caster sugar
2 medium eggs
150g (5oz) self-raising flour, sifted
1 tbsp milk
zest of 1 lemon
50g (2oz) small fresh blueberries
12 fresh raspberries

For the frosting
1 medium egg white
175g (6oz) caster sugar
a pinch of cream of tartar

1 Preheat the oven to 190°C (170°C fan oven) mark 5. Line a 12-hole muffin tin with paper fairy cake or bun cases.

2 Using a hand-held electric whisk, whisk the butter and sugar in a bowl, or beat with a wooden spoon, until pale and creamy. Gradually whisk in the eggs until just combined. Using a metal spoon, fold in the flour, milk, lemon zest and blueberries until combined.

3 Divide the mixture equally between the paper cases and press 1 raspberry into the centre of each cake. Bake for 15 minutes or until golden and risen. Leave to cool in the tin for 5 minutes, then transfer to a wire rack to cool completely.

4 For the frosting, put the egg white, caster sugar, 2 tbsp water and cream of tartar into a heatproof bowl and whisk lightly using a hand-held electric whisk. Put the bowl over a pan of simmering water and whisk continuously for about 7 minutes or until the mixture thickens sufficiently to stand in peaks.

5 Insert a star nozzle into a piping bag, then fill the bag with the frosting and pipe a swirl on to the top of each cake. Stand the cakes upright on the wire rack and leave for about 1 hour to set.

Sour Cherry Cupcakes

Makes 12

Preparation Time
30 minutes

Cooking Time
15–20 minutes,
plus cooling
and setting

Per Cupcake
323 calories
14g fat
(of which 8g saturates)
50g carbohydrate
0.4g salt

175g (6oz) unsalted butter, softened
175g (6oz) golden caster sugar
3 medium eggs
175g (6oz) self-raising flour, sifted
75g (3oz) dried cherries
2 tbsp milk

For the icing
225g (8oz) golden icing sugar,
sifted
3 tbsp lemon juice, strained

1 Preheat the oven to 190°C (170°C fan oven) mark 5. Line a 12-hole bun tin or muffin tin with paper muffin cases.

2 Put the butter and caster sugar into a bowl and cream together until pale, light and fluffy. Beat in the eggs, one at a time, folding in 1 tbsp flour if the mixture looks like it is starting to curdle.

3 Put 12 dried cherries to one side. Fold the remaining flour, the cherries and milk into the creamed mixture until evenly combined. Spoon the mixture into the paper cases and bake for 15–20 minutes until pale golden and risen. Transfer to a wire rack to cool completely.

4 Put the icing sugar into a bowl and mix with the lemon juice to make a smooth dropping consistency. Spoon a little icing on to each cake and decorate each with a cherry, then stand the cakes upright on the wire rack and leave for about 1 hour to set.

Brazil Nut & Clementine Cakes

Makes 8
Preparation Time
30 minutes,
plus cooling
and freezing
Cooking Time
1¼ hours,
plus cooling

Per Cake
413 calories
26g fat
(of which 5g saturates)
41g carbohydrate
0.1g salt

butter to grease
1 lemon
10 clementines
150g (5oz) brazil nuts
100ml (3½fl oz) mild olive oil
3 medium eggs
275g (10oz) golden caster sugar
1 tsp baking powder
2 tbsp brandy

To decorate
mint sprigs
icing sugar

1 Grease eight 150ml (¼ pint) ramekin dishes and baseline with greaseproof paper. Wash the lemon and 4 clementines and put into a pan. Cover with boiling water, reduce the heat to a gentle simmer and cook for 30 minutes or until the clementines are tender.

2 Remove the clementines with a slotted spoon and set aside. Cook the lemon for a further 10 minutes or until tender. Drain, reserving 200ml (7fl oz) liquid, and cool slightly. Halve the fruit, remove the pips and roughly chop.

3 Preheat the oven to 180°C (160°C fan oven) mark 4. Grind the nuts in a food processor until finely chopped, then tip out and set aside. There's no need to wash the jug – add the cooked fruit and blend to a purée.

4 Put the oil, eggs and 125g (4oz) caster sugar into a mixing bowl and whisk until slightly thick and foamy. Stir in the ground nuts, fruit purée and baking powder. Divide among the ramekins. put on a baking sheet. Bake for 25 minutes or until slightly risen and firm to the touch. Leave to cool in the tin.

5 Peel the remaining clementines, remove the pips and divide into segments, then skin each segment. Heat the remaining sugar in a small pan with 150ml (¼ pint) of the reserved cooking liquid until the sugar dissolves. Bring to the boil and cook until a pale caramel in colour. Dip the base of the pan into cold water to stop the caramel cooking. Stir in the remaining liquid and the brandy. Return to the heat, stirring until the caramel has dissolved. Stir in the clementine segments.

6 Loosen the edges of the cakes, turn out on to individual plates and remove the paper lining. Pile the fruit segments on top and spoon the caramel over them. Decorate each with a mint sprig and a dusting of icing sugar.

Get Ahead
Make the recipe to the end of step 5. Wrap the cakes, still in their ramekins, in clingfilm and pour the clementines and syrup into a freezerproof bag. You can freeze both for up to one month.
To use Thaw the cakes at room temperature for 4 hours or overnight in the fridge. Finish with step 6.

St Clements Cupcakes

Makes 9
Preparation Time
40 minutes
Cooking Time
15–18 minutes,
plus cooling
and setting

Per Cupcake
309 calories
1g fat
(of which trace saturates)
76g carbohydrate
0g salt

1 small orange (about 200g/7oz)
175g (6oz) self-raising flour, sifted
100g (3½oz) caster sugar
100ml (3½fl oz) milk
1 medium egg, beaten
50g (2oz) unsalted butter, melted
1 tsp baking powder
zest of 1 large lemon

For the topping and decoration
400g (14oz) royal icing sugar, sifted
juice and zest of 1 small orange
sugar star sprinkles
edible glitter (optional)

1 Preheat the oven to 190°C (170°C fan oven) mark 5. Line a 12-hole muffin tin with 9 paper muffin cases.

2 Grate the zest from the orange into a large bowl and set aside. Cut the top and bottom off the orange and stand it upright on a board. Using a serrated knife, cut away the pith in a downward motion. Roughly chop the orange flesh, discarding any pips. Put the chopped orange into a food processor and whiz until puréed.

3 Transfer the orange purée into the bowl with the zest. Add the flour, caster sugar, milk, egg, melted butter, baking powder and lemon zest. Stir with a spatula until just combined. Divide the mixture equally between the paper cases.

4 Bake for 15–18 minutes until golden and risen. Leave to cool in the tin for 5 minutes, then transfer to a wire rack to cool completely.

5 For the topping, put the icing sugar, orange juice and zest into a bowl and whisk for 5 minutes or until soft peaks form. Spoon a little over the top of each cake to flood the top, then sprinkle with the stars. Stand the cakes upright on the wire rack and leave for about 1 hour to set. Dust with edible glitter, if you like, when set.

The Ultimate Carrot Cupcakes

Makes 12
Preparation Time
30 minutes
Cooking Time
20 minutes,
plus cooling

Per Cupcake
255 calories
12g fat
(of which 4g saturates)
34g carbohydrate
0.3g salt

150g (5oz) carrots
50g (2oz) raisins
175g (6oz) self-raising flour, sifted
½ tsp bicarbonate of soda
150g (5oz) light soft brown sugar
zest of 1 orange
½ tsp ground mixed spice
3 medium eggs
100ml (3½fl oz) sunflower oil
75ml (2½fl oz) buttermilk

For the topping and decoration
50g (2oz) icing sugar, sifted
250g (9oz) mascarpone cheese
100g (3½oz) quark cheese
juice of ½ orange
red, yellow and green ready-made fondant icing (optional)

1 Preheat the oven to 190°C (170°C fan oven) mark 5. Line a 12-hole muffin tin with paper muffin cases.

2 Coarsely grate the carrots and put into a large bowl. Add the raisins, flour, bicarbonate of soda, brown sugar, orange zest and mixed spice. Put the eggs, oil and buttermilk into a jug and lightly beat together until combined. Pour the egg mixture into the flour and stir with a spatula until just combined.

3 Divide the mixture equally between the paper cases and bake for 20 minutes or until lightly golden and risen. Leave to cool in the tin for 5 minutes, then transfer to a wire rack to cool completely.

4 For the topping, mix the sifted icing sugar with the mascarpone, quark and orange juice to a smooth icing. Using a small palette knife, spread a little of the icing over each cake. Use the coloured fondant to make small carrots, if you like, and use to decorate the cakes.

Forest Fruit Cupcakes

Makes 12
Preparation Time
25 minutes
Cooking Time
18–20 minutes,
plus cooling

Per cupcake:
506 calories
27g fat
(of which 17g saturates);
66g carbohydrate
(54g total sugars)

175g (6oz) caster sugar
175g (6oz) unsalted butter, at room temperature
3 medium eggs, lightly beaten
Finely grated zest of 1 lemon
175g (6oz) plain flour, sifted
1 tsp baking powder
100g (3½oz) seedless dark jam
(we used blackcurrant)

For the icing
200g (7oz) unsalted butter, at room temperature
1 tsp vanilla extract
375g (13oz) icing sugar, sifted
50g (2oz) fresh blackberries

1 Preheat the oven to 180°C (160°C fan) mark 4. Line a 12-hole muffin tin with paper muffin cases.

2 Using a hand-held electric whisk, beat the caster sugar and butter in a large bowl for 3 minutes or until light and fluffy. Gradually add the eggs, whisking continuously – if the mixture looks as if it is about to curdle, add 1 tbsp flour. Whisk in half of the lemon zest.

3 Use a large metal spoon to fold in the flour and baking powder. Divide the mixture evenly between the paper cases and bake for 18–20 minutes until golden. Transfer to a wire rack to cool completely.

4 Spoon the jam into a piping bag fitted with a 5–7mm (about ¼in) plain nozzle. Push the piping nozzle into the middle of the top of each cake and squeeze a little jam into the centre.

5 For the icing, put the butter, vanilla, the remaining lemon zest and ⅔ of the icing sugar into a large bowl and slowly beat with a hand-held electric whisk. Gradually beat in the remaining icing sugar until you have a soft but spreadable consistency that holds its shape. Briefly whisk in the fresh blackberries to get a marbled effect.

6 Pipe or spread the icing on to the cakes and serve.

GET AHEAD
Prepare up to the end of step 3 up to a day ahead. Leave to cool completely, then transfer the cakes to an airtight container and store at room temperature.
To use Complete the recipe to serve.

Apple Crumble Cupcakes

Makes 12
Preparation Time
20 minutes
Cooking Time
25 minutes,
plus cooling

Per Cupcake
215 calories
10g fat
(of which 6g saturates)
31g carbohydrate
0.2g salt

320g (11½oz) eating apples, cored (about 2)
juice of 1 lemon
200g (7oz) self-raising flour, sifted
1 tsp baking powder
1 tsp ground cinnamon
125g (4oz) light soft brown sugar
2 medium eggs
100g (3½oz) unsalted butter, melted

For the crumble
50g (2oz) plain flour
25g (1oz) unsalted butter, chilled and cut into cubes
15g (½oz) light soft brown sugar

1 Preheat the oven to 180°C (160°C fan oven) mark 4. Line a 12-hole muffin tin with paper muffin cases.

2 Make the crumble. Put the flour into a large bowl and, using your fingertips, rub in the butter until it resembles coarse breadcrumbs. Stir in the sugar and set aside.

3 Coarsely grate the apples into a large bowl and mix in the lemon juice. Add the flour, baking powder, cinnamon and sugar. Put the eggs and melted butter into a jug and lightly beat together, then pour into the flour mixture. Stir with a spatula until just combined. Divide the mixture equally between the paper cases, then sprinkle the crumble equally over the top of each cake.

4 Bake for 25 minutes or until lightly golden and risen. Leave to cool in the tin for 5 minutes, then transfer to a wire rack to cool completely.

Raspberry Ripple Cupcakes

Makes 9
Preparation Time
30 minutes
Cooking Time
20 minutes,
plus cooling

Per Cupcake
385 calories
26g fat
(of which 16g saturates)
36g carbohydrate
0.5g salt

50g (2oz) seedless raspberry jam
50g (2oz) fresh raspberries
125g (4oz) unsalted butter, softened
100g (3½oz) caster sugar
2 medium eggs
1 tbsp milk
150g (5oz) self-raising flour, sifted

For the topping and decoration
150g (5oz) fresh raspberries
300ml (½ pint) whipping cream
50g (2oz) icing sugar, sifted

1 Preheat the oven to 190°C (170°C fan oven) mark 5. Line a 12-hole muffin tin with paper muffin cases.

2 Mix the raspberry jam with the raspberries, lightly crushing the raspberries. Set aside.

3 Using a hand-held electric whisk, whisk the butter and caster sugar in a bowl, or beat with a wooden spoon, until pale and creamy. Gradually whisk in the eggs and milk until just combined. Using a metal spoon, fold in the flour until just combined, then carefully fold in the raspberry jam mixture until just marbled, being careful not to over-mix. Divide the mixture equally between the paper cases.

4 Bake for 20 minutes or until golden and risen. Leave to cool in the tin for 5 minutes, then transfer to a wire rack to cool completely.

5 For the topping, reserve 9 raspberries. Mash the remaining raspberries in a bowl with a fork. Pass through a sieve into a bowl to remove the seeds. Using a hand-held electric whisk, whip the cream and icing sugar together until stiff peaks form. Mix the raspberry purée into the cream until combined.

6 Insert a star nozzle into a piping bag, then fill the bag with the cream and pipe a swirl on to the top of each cake. Decorate each with a raspberry.

Coconut & Lime Cupcakes

Makes 12
Preparation Time
30 minutes
Cooking Time
18–20 minutes,
plus cooling
and setting

Per Cupcake
291 calories
13g fat
(of which 6g saturates)
42g carbohydrate
0.1g salt

275g (10oz) plain flour, sifted
1 tbsp baking powder
100g (3½oz) caster sugar
zest of 1 lime
50g (2oz) desiccated coconut
2 medium eggs
100ml (3½fl oz) sunflower oil
225ml (8fl oz) natural yogurt
50ml (2fl oz) milk

For the topping
150g (5oz) icing sugar, sifted
juice of 1 lime
50g (2oz) desiccated coconut

1 Preheat the oven to 200°C (180°C fan oven) mark 6. Line a 12-hole muffin tin with paper muffin cases.

2 Put the flour, baking powder, caster sugar, lime zest and coconut into a large bowl. Put the eggs, oil, yogurt and milk into a jug and lightly beat together until combined. Pour the yogurt mixture into the flour and stir with a spatula until just combined. Divide the mixture equally between the paper cases.

3 Bake for 18–20 minutes until lightly golden and risen. Leave to cool in the tin for 5 minutes, then transfer to a wire rack to cool completely.

4 For the topping, mix the icing sugar with the lime juice and 1–2 tsp boiling water to make a thick, smooth icing. Put the coconut into a shallow bowl. Dip each cake top into the icing until coated, allowing the excess to drip off, then carefully dip into the coconut until coated. Stand the cakes upright on the wire rack and leave for about 1 hour to set.

Orange & Poppy Seed Cupcakes

Makes 12
Preparation Time
30 minutes
Cooking Time
20 minutes,
plus cooling

Per Cupcake
408 calories
24g fat
(of which 14g saturates)
49g carbohydrate
0.5g salt

175g (6oz) unsalted butter, softened
175g (6oz) caster sugar
3 medium eggs
175g (6oz) self-raising flour, sifted
grated zest and juice of 1 large orange
2 tbsp poppy seeds
1 tsp baking powder

For the icing and decoration
125g (4oz) unsalted butter, softened
250g (9oz) icing sugar, sifted
1 tbsp orange flower water
12 orange jelly slices and orange
edible glitter (optional)

1 Preheat the oven to 190°C (170°C fan oven) mark 5. Line a 12-hole muffin tin with paper muffin cases.

2 Whisk the butter and caster sugar in a bowl with a hand-held electric whisk, or beat with a wooden spoon, until pale and creamy. Gradually whisk in the eggs until just combined. Using a metal spoon, fold in the flour, orange zest and juice, poppy seeds and baking powder until combined. Divide the mixture equally between the paper cases.

3 Bake for 20 minutes or until golden and risen. Leave to cool in the tin for 5 minutes, then transfer to a wire rack to cool completely.

4 For the icing, put the butter into a bowl and whisk until fluffy. Gradually add the icing sugar and orange flower water and whisk until light and fluffy.

5 Insert a star nozzle into a piping bag, then fill the bag with the buttercream and pipe a swirl on to the top of each cake. Decorate each with an orange slice and edible glitter, if you like.

Ginger & Orange Cupcakes

Makes 12

Preparation Time
15 minutes

Cooking Time
20 minutes,
plus cooling
and setting

Per Cupcake
309 calories
14g fat
(of which 8g saturates)
46g carbohydrate
0.4g salt

175g (6oz) unsalted butter, softened
175g (6oz) golden caster sugar
3 medium eggs
175g (6oz) self-raising flour, sifted
finely grated zest and juice of 1 orange
2 pieces of drained and chopped preserved stem
ginger, plus 1 piece extra for decoration

For the icing and decoration
225g (8oz) icing sugar, sifted
2–3 tbsp orange juice, strained

1 Preheat the oven to 190°C (170°C fan oven) mark 5. Line a 12-hole muffin tin with paper muffin cases.

2 Put the butter and caster sugar into a bowl and beat with a hand-held electric whisk until pale, light and fluffy. Add the eggs, one at a time, and beat together, folding 1 tbsp flour into the mixture if it looks as if it is about to curdle. Fold in the flour, orange zest and juice and stem ginger and mix well.

3 Divide the mixture equally between the paper cases and bake for 15–20 minutes until pale golden, risen and springy to the touch. Transfer to a wire rack to cool completely.

4 For the icing, put the icing sugar into a large bowl and mix in the orange juice to make a smooth dropping consistency. Spoon the icing on to the cakes, then decorate with finely chopped stem ginger. Stand the cakes on the wire rack and leave for about 1 hour to set.

Be Mine Cupcakes

Makes 12

Preparation Time
30 minutes

Cooking Time
15 minutes,
plus cooling

Per Cupcake
289 calories
15g fat
(of which 9g saturates)
40g carbohydrate
0.3g salt

125g (4oz) unsalted butter, softened
100g (3½oz) caster sugar
2 medium eggs
125g (4oz) self-raising flour, sifted
½ tsp baking powder
1 × 51g bar Turkish Delight, finely chopped
1 tbsp rosewater

For the topping and decoration
75g (3oz) unsalted butter, softened
250g (9oz) icing sugar, sifted
2 tbsp rosewater
pink and white heart-shaped sugar sprinkles
about 12 Loveheart sweets (optional)

1 Preheat the oven to 190°C (170°C fan oven) mark 5. Line a 12-hole muffin tin with paper fairy cake cases.

2 Using a hand-held electric whisk, whisk the butter and caster sugar in a bowl, or beat with a wooden spoon, until pale and creamy. Gradually whisk in the eggs until just combined. Using a metal spoon, fold in the flour, baking powder, Turkish Delight and rosewater until combined. Divide the mixture equally between the paper cases.

3 Bake for 15 minutes or until golden and risen. Leave to cool in the tin for 5 minutes, then transfer to a wire rack to cool completely.

4 For the topping, put the butter into a bowl and whisk until fluffy. Add the icing sugar and rosewater and whisk until light and fluffy. Using a small palette knife, spread a little buttercream over the top of each cake. Decorate with sugar hearts, then top each with a Loveheart, if you like.

Sweet Shop Cupcakes

Makes 12
Preparation Time
30 minutes
Cooking Time
20 minutes,
plus cooling
and setting

Per Cupcake
424 calories
19g fat
(of which 12g saturates)
64g carbohydrate
0.6g salt

175g (6oz) unsalted butter, softened
175g (6oz) caster sugar
3 medium eggs
175g (6oz) self-raising flour, sifted
zest of 1 lemon
½ tsp baking powder
125g (4oz) lemon curd

For the topping and decoration
75g (3oz) unsalted butter, softened
350g (12oz) icing sugar, sifted
50ml (2fl oz) milk
dolly mixtures, jelly beans or
chocolate buttons

1 Preheat the oven to 190°C (170°C fan oven) mark 5. Line a 12-hole muffin tin with paper muffin cases.

2 Using a hand-held electric whisk, whisk the butter and caster sugar in a bowl, or beat with a wooden spoon, until pale and creamy. Gradually whisk in the eggs until just combined. Using a metal spoon, fold in the flour, lemon zest and baking powder until combined. Divide the mixture equally between the paper cases.

3 Bake for 20 minutes or until golden and risen. Leave to cool in the tin for 5 minutes, then transfer to a wire rack to cool completely.

4 Cut a small cone shape from the top of each cake. Put a teaspoonful of lemon curd into the hole in each cake and then replace the cake cone, pressing down lightly.

5 For the topping, put the butter into a bowl and whisk until fluffy. Gradually add half the icing sugar, whisking until combined. Add the milk and remaining icing sugar and whisk until light and fluffy, then, using a small palette knife, spread a little over each cake. Stand the cakes upright on the wire rack and leave for about 30 minutes to set. Decorate each cake with sweets when set.

Rocky Road Cupcakes

Makes 9	100g (3½oz) unsalted butter, softened
Preparation Time	125g (4oz) caster sugar
30 minutes	2 medium eggs
Cooking Time	150g (5oz) self-raising flour, sifted
15–20 minutes,	25g (1oz) glacé cherries, diced
plus cooling	25g (1oz) milk chocolate chips
and setting	25g (1oz) pinenuts
Per Cupcake	**For the topping**
360 calories	100g (3½oz) milk chocolate
20g fat	50ml (2fl oz) double cream
(of which 11g saturates)	25g (1oz) mini marshmallows
45g carbohydrate	25g (1oz) glacé cherries, finely chopped
0.5g salt	1 × 37g bag Maltesers

1 Preheat the oven to 190°C (170°C fan oven) mark 5. Line a 12-hole muffin tin with 9 paper muffin cases.

2 Using a hand-held electric whisk, whisk the butter and sugar in a bowl, or beat with a wooden spoon, until pale and creamy. Gradually whisk in the eggs until just combined. Using a metal spoon, fold in the flour, cherries, chocolate chips and pinenuts until combined. Divide the mixture equally between the paper cases.

3 Bake for 15–20 minutes until golden and risen. Leave to cool in the tin for 5 minutes, then transfer to a wire rack to cool completely.

4 For the topping, break the chocolate into pieces, then put into a heatproof bowl with the cream. Set over a pan of gently simmering water, making sure the base of the bowl doesn't touch the water. Heat until melted, stirring occasionally until smooth.

5 Remove from the heat and, using a small palette knife, spread a little over the top of each cake. Decorate each with marshmallows, cherries and Maltesers. Stand the cakes upright on the wire rack and leave for about 1 hour to set.

Mallow Madness Cupcakes

Makes 12
Preparation Time
40 minutes
Cooking Time
20–25 minutes,
plus cooling
and setting

Per Cupcake
317 calories
13g fat
(of which 2g saturates)
49g carbohydrate
0.1g salt

3 medium eggs
175g (6oz) self-raising flour, sifted
150g (5oz) caster sugar
175ml (6fl oz) sunflower oil
½ tsp baking powder
50g (2oz) white chocolate chips

For the topping and decoration
125g (4oz) pink and white marshmallows
1 medium egg white
150g (5oz) caster sugar
a pinch of cream of tartar
pink sugar sprinkles

1 Preheat the oven to 190°C (170°C fan oven) mark 5. Line a 12-hole muffin tin with paper muffin cases.

2 Put the eggs, flour, sugar, oil and baking powder into a large bowl and, using a hand-held electric whisk, whisk until just combined. Add the chocolate chips and fold through. Divide the mixture equally between the paper cases.

3 Bake for 20–25 minutes until lightly golden and risen. Leave to cool in the tin for 5 minutes, then transfer to a wire rack to cool completely.

4 For the topping, reserve 6 white marshmallows. Put the remaining marshmallows, the egg white, sugar and a pinch of cream of tartar into a heatproof bowl and whisk lightly using a hand-held electric whisk. Put the bowl over a pan of simmering water and whisk continuously, for about 7 minutes or until the marshmallows have melted and the mixture thickens sufficiently to stand in peaks.

5 Cut the reserved marshmallows in half. Spread a little of the icing over the top of each cake. Scatter with sugar sprinkles and top each with a marshmallow half. Stand the cakes upright on the wire rack and leave for about 1 hour to set.

Coffee Walnut Whip Cupcakes

Makes 12	100g (3½oz) walnuts
Preparation Time	175g (6oz) unsalted butter, softened
30 minutes	150g (5oz) self-raising flour, sifted
Cooking Time	175g (6oz) light soft brown sugar
20–25 minutes,	3 medium eggs
plus cooling	1 tsp baking powder
and chilling	50ml (2fl oz) milk
Per Cupcake	**For the topping and decoration**
409 calories	1 tbsp instant coffee granules
26g fat	50g (2oz) unsalted butter, softened
(of which 11g saturates)	200g (7oz) icing sugar, sifted
43g carbohydrate	50g (2oz) walnuts, finely chopped
0.5g salt	

1 Preheat the oven to 190°C (170°C fan oven) mark 5. Line a 12-hole muffin tin with paper muffin cases.

2 Whiz the walnuts in a food processor until finely ground. Transfer to a large bowl. Add the butter, flour, brown sugar, eggs, baking powder and milk to the ground walnuts. Using a hand-held electric whisk, whisk together until pale and creamy. Divide the mixture equally between the paper cases.

3 Bake for 20–25 minutes until golden and risen. Leave to cool in the tin for 5 minutes, then transfer to a wire rack to cool completely.

4 For the buttercream topping, put 2 tbsp boiling water into a small bowl, add the coffee and stir to dissolve. Put the butter, 100g (3½oz) icing sugar and the coffee mixture into a bowl and whisk until combined. Chill for 30 minutes.

5 Remove the buttercream from the fridge and gradually whisk in the remaining icing sugar until smooth and fluffy. Using a small palette knife, spread a little buttercream over the top of each cake. Put the chopped walnuts into a shallow bowl and lightly dip the top of each cake into the walnuts.

Banoffee Cupcakes

Makes 12
Preparation Time
30 minutes
Cooking Time
20 minutes,
plus cooling

Per Cupcake
404 calories
16g fat
(of which 10g saturates)
63g carbohydrate
0.4g salt

175g (6oz) self-raising flour, sifted
½ tsp bicarbonate of soda
150g (5oz) light soft brown sugar
1 banana (about 150g/5oz), peeled
3 medium eggs
100g (3½oz) unsalted butter, melted
75ml (2½fl oz) buttermilk

For the topping and decoration
150g (5oz) dulce de leche toffee sauce
75g (3oz) unsalted butter, softened
250g (9oz) golden icing sugar, sifted
mini fudge chunks (optional)

1 Preheat the oven to 190°C (170°C fan oven) mark 5. Line a 12-hole muffin tin with paper muffin cases.

2 Put the flour, bicarbonate of soda and brown sugar into a large bowl. Mash the banana with a fork in a small bowl. Put the eggs, melted butter and buttermilk into a jug and lightly beat together until combined. Pour into the flour mixture along with the mashed banana and stir with a spatula until just combined. Divide the mixture equally between the paper cases.

3 Bake for 18–20 minutes until lightly golden and risen. Leave to cool in the tin for 5 minutes, then transfer to a wire rack to cool completely.

4 For the topping, whisk together the dulce de leche and butter in a bowl until combined. Gradually whisk in the icing sugar until light and fluffy. Use a palette knife to spread the buttercream on to the top of each cake. Decorate with the mini fudge chunks, if using.

Black Forest Cupcakes

Makes 12
Preparation Time
15 minutes
Cooking Time
20 minutes,
plus cooling

Per Cupcake
350 calories
21g fat
(of which 9g saturates)
39g carbohydrate
0.4g salt

85g (3oz) self-raising flour
4 tbsp cocoa powder
1 tsp baking powder
125g (4oz) caster sugar
125g (4oz) soft margarine or butter
2 large eggs

For the topping and decoration
1 × 250g jar black cherry jam
200 ml (7fl oz) double cream, whipped
50g (2oz) dark chocolate (at least 70%
cocoa solids), grated
glacé cherries, to decorate (optional)

1 Preheat the oven to 190°C (170°C fan oven) mark 5. Line a 12-hole muffin tin with paper muffin cases.

2 Sift the flour, cocoa powder, baking powder and sugar into a large bowl, food processor or mixer. Add the margarine and eggs and beat well until the mixture is pale and creamy.

3 Divide the mixture equally between the paper cases and bake for about 20 minutes or until firm to the touch. Transfer to a wire rack to cool completely.

4 For the topping, cover the top of each cupcake with a generous amount of the jam – or you can use a jar of cherries that have been soaked in kirsch, if you like. Add the whipped cream and decorate with grated dark chocolate and a glacé cherry.

Cookies & Cream Cupcakes

Makes 12
Preparation Time
30 minutes
Cooking Time
15–20 minutes,
plus cooling

Per Cupcake
357 calories
21g fat
(of which 13g saturates)
41g carbohydrate
0.5g salt

75g (3oz) mini Oreo cookies
175g (6oz) unsalted butter, softened
150g (5oz) caster sugar
3 medium eggs
175g (6oz) self-raising flour, sifted
½ tsp baking powder
3 tbsp milk
½ tsp vanilla extract

For the topping
75g (3oz) unsalted butter, softened
150g (5oz) icing sugar, sifted
2 tsp vanilla extract
1 tsp cocoa powder

1 Preheat the oven to 200°C (180°C fan oven) mark 6. Line a 12-hole muffin tin with paper muffin cases. Reserve 12 mini cookies and roughly chop the remainder.

2 Using a hand-held electric whisk, whisk the butter and caster sugar in a bowl (or beat with a wooden spoon) until pale and creamy. Gradually whisk in the eggs until just combined. Using a metal spoon, fold in the flour, baking powder, milk, vanilla extract and chopped cookies until combined. Divide the mixture equally between the paper cases.

3 Bake for 15–20 minutes until golden and risen. Leave to cool in the tin for 5 minutes, then transfer to a wire rack to cool completely.

4 For the topping, put the butter into a bowl and whisk until fluffy. Gradually add the icing sugar and vanilla extract and whisk until light and fluffy. Using a small palette knife, spread the buttercream over the top of each cake. Sift a little cocoa powder on to the top of each cake and then decorate each with a reserved Oreo cookie.

Polka Dot Cupcakes

Makes 12
Preparation Time
30 minutes
Cooking Time
20 minutes,
plus cooling

Per Cupcake
283 calories
12g fat
(of which 4g saturates)
42g carbohydrate
0.2g salt

250g (9oz) plain flour, sifted
1 tbsp baking powder
100g (3½oz) caster sugar
1 tbsp vanilla extract
2 medium eggs
125ml (4fl oz) sunflower oil
175g (6oz) natural yogurt

For the topping and decoration
50g (2oz) unsalted butter, softened
175g (6oz) icing sugar, sifted
25g (1oz) cocoa powder, sifted
mini Smarties or chocolate beans

1 Preheat the oven to 190°C (170°C fan oven) mark 5. Line a 12-hole muffin tin with paper muffin cases.

2 Put the flour, baking powder and caster sugar into a large bowl. Put the vanilla extract, eggs, oil and yogurt into a jug and lightly beat together until combined. Pour into the flour mixture and stir with a spatula until just combined. Divide the mixture equally between the paper cases.

3 Bake for 20 minutes or until lightly golden and risen. Leave to cool in the tin for 5 minutes, then transfer to a wire rack to cool completely.

4 For the topping, put the butter into a bowl and whisk until fluffy. Gradually add the icing sugar until combined. Add the cocoa powder and 2 tbsp boiling water and whisk until light and fluffy. Using a small palette knife, spread a little buttercream over the top of each cake. Decorate with mini Smarties or chocolate beans.

Marbled Chocolate Cupcakes

Makes 12
Preparation Time
40 minutes
Cooking Time
20 minutes,
plus cooling

Per Cupcake
360 calories
16g fat
(of which 10g saturates)
54g carbohydrate
0.5g salt

75g (3oz) unsalted butter, softened
150g (5oz) caster sugar
2 medium eggs
25g (1oz) self-raising flour, sifted
125g (4oz) plain flour, sifted
½ tsp bicarbonate of soda
2 tsp vanilla extract
150ml (¼ pint) buttermilk
25g (1oz) cocoa powder, sifted

For the topping
125g (4oz) unsalted butter, softened
350g (12oz) icing sugar, sifted
2 tsp vanilla extract
2 tbsp cocoa powder, sifted

1 Preheat the oven to 190°C (170°C fan oven) mark 5. Line a 12-hole muffin tin with paper muffin cases.

2 Using a hand-held electric whisk, whisk the butter and caster sugar in a bowl, or beat with a wooden spoon, until pale and creamy. Gradually whisk in the eggs until just combined. Using a metal spoon, fold in both flours, the bicarbonate of soda, vanilla extract and buttermilk until combined. Put half this mixture into another bowl and whisk in the cocoa powder. Then very lightly fold this mixture into the vanilla mixture, to create a marbled effect. Divide the mixture equally between the paper cases.

3 Bake for 20 minutes or until golden and risen. Leave to cool in the tin for 5 minutes, then transfer to a wire rack to cool completely.

4 For the topping, put the butter into a bowl and whisk until fluffy. Gradually whisk in half the icing sugar, then add the vanilla extract, 2 tbsp boiling water and the remaining icing sugar and whisk until light and fluffy. Put half the mixture into another bowl and whisk in the cocoa powder.

5 Insert a star nozzle into a piping bag, then fill the bag alternately with the vanilla and chocolate buttercreams. Pipe a swirl on to the top of each cake.

Chocolate Cupcakes

Makes 18
Preparation Time
15 minutes
Cooking Time
20 minutes,
plus cooling
and setting

Per Cupcake
203 calories
14g fat
(of which 8g saturates)
19g carbohydrate
0.2g salt

125g (4oz) unsalted butter, softened
125g (4oz) light muscovado sugar
2 medium eggs, beaten
15g (½oz) cocoa powder
100g (3½oz) self-raising flour
100g (3½oz) plain chocolate (at least 70%
cocoa solids), roughly chopped

For the topping
150ml (¼ pint) double cream
100g (3½oz) plain chocolate (at least 70%
cocoa solids), broken into pieces

1 Preheat the oven to 190°C (170°C fan oven) mark 5. Line a 12-hole and a 6-hole bun tin or muffin tin with paper muffin cases.

2 Beat the butter and sugar together until light and fluffy. Gradually beat in the eggs. Sift the cocoa powder with the flour and fold into the creamed mixture with the chopped chocolate. Divide the mixture equally between the paper cases and lightly flatten the surface with the back of a spoon.

3 Bake for 20 minutes, then transfer to a wire rack to cool completely.

4 For the topping, put the cream and chocolate into a heavy-based pan over a low heat and heat until melted, then leave to cool and thicken slightly. Spoon on to the cooled cakes, then stand the cakes upright on the wire rack and leave for 30 minutes to set.

Fairy Cakes

**Makes 18 fairy cakes
or 12 cupcakes**

Preparation Time

20 minutes

Cooking Time

10–15 minutes,
plus cooling
and setting

Per Cake

160 calories
6g fat
(of which 4g saturates)
26g carbohydrate
0.2g salt

125g (4oz) self-raising flour, sifted
1 tsp baking powder
125g (4oz) caster sugar
125g (4oz) unsalted butter, very soft
2 medium eggs
1 tbsp milk

For the icing and decoration
225g (8oz) icing sugar, sifted
assorted food colourings (optional)
sweets, sprinkles or coloured sugar

1 Preheat the oven to 200°C (180°C fan oven) mark 6.
Put paper cases into 18 of the holes in two bun tins.

2 Put the flour, baking powder, sugar, butter, eggs and
milk into a mixing bowl and beat with a hand-held
electric whisk for 2 minutes or until the mixture is pale
and very soft. Half-fill each paper case with the mixture.

3 Bake for 10–15 minutes until golden brown. Transfer
to a wire rack to cool completely.

4 For the icing, put the icing sugar into a bowl and
gradually blend in 2–3 tbsp warm water until the
icing is fairly stiff, but spreadable. Add a couple of drops
of food colouring, if you like.

5 Spread the tops of the cakes with the icing and
decorate with sweets, sprinkles or coloured sugar.

Chocolate Butterfly Cakes

Serves 18

Preparation Time
25 minutes

Cooking Time
15-20 minutes,
plus cooling

125g (4oz) unsalted butter, very soft
125g (4oz) caster sugar
2 medium eggs, lightly beaten individually
125g (4oz) plain flour
25g (1oz) cocoa powder
½ tsp baking powder
1 tbsp milk

Per Cake
170 calories
7g fat
(of which 4g saturates)
26g carbohydrate
0.2g salt

For the icing and decoration
1 × quantity of buttercream icing (see below)

1 Preheat the oven to 190°C (170°C fan oven) mark 5. Put 18 cake cases into 2 bun trays.

2 Using a hand-held electric whisk, beat the butter and sugar together until soft and fluffy and lighter in colour. Beat in the eggs thoroughly, one at a time.

3 Sift the flour, cocoa powder and baking powder into the bowl and fold in gently until well mixed. Fold in the milk to give a soft, dropping consistency. Divide the mixture equally between the paper cases.

4 Bake for 15-20 minutes until risen and firm. Transfer to a wire rack to cool completely.

5 Slice off the top of each cake and cut the slice in half. Using a palette knife, spread buttercream on each cake. Put the 'butterfly wings' on top, with their curved sides facing towards each other.

Cook's Tip
Colour the buttercream with pink or green food colouring if you like, to match the theme of the party.

Buttercream

75g (3oz) unsalted butter, softened
175g (6oz) icing sugar, sifted
a few drops of vanilla extract
1-2 tbsp milk or water

Put the butter into a bowl and beat with a wooden spoon or hand-held electric whisk until pale and creamy. Gradually stir in the icing sugar, followed by the vanilla and milk or water. Beat well until light and smooth. Either use immediately or cover well with clingfilm to exclude air.

Chocolate Fairy Cakes

Makes 18
Preparation Time
20 minutes
Cooking Time
10–15 minutes,
plus cooling
and setting

Per Cupcake
171 calories
7g fat
(of which 4g saturates)
28g carbohydrate
0.3g salt

100g (3½oz) self-raising flour
25g (1oz) cocoa powder
1 tsp baking powder
125g (4oz) caster sugar
125g (4oz) unsalted butter, very soft
2 medium eggs
1 tbsp milk
50g (2oz) chocolate drops

For the icing and decoration
225g (8oz) icing sugar, sifted
assorted food colourings (optional)
sweets, sprinkles or coloured sugar

1 Preheat the oven to 200°C (180°C fan oven) mark 6. Put paper cases into 18 of the holes in two bun tins.

2 Sift the flour into a mixing bowl, then sift in the cocoa powder, baking powder and sugar. Add the butter, eggs and milk and beat with a hand-held electric whisk for 2 minutes or until the mixture is pale and very soft. Stir in the chocolate drops, and spoon into into the cases.

3 Bake for 10–15 minutes until risen and spingy to the touch. Transfer to a wire rack to cool completely.

4 For the icing, put the icing sugar into a bowl and gradually blend in 2–3 tbsp warm water until the icing is fairly stiff, but spreadable. Add a couple of drops of food colouring, if you like.

5 Spread the tops of the cakes with the icing and decorate with sweets, sprinkles or coloured sugar.

Kitten Cupcakes

Makes 12
Preparation Time
25 minutes
Cooking Time
20 minutes,
plus cooling

Per Cupcake
223 calories
10g fat
(of which 6g saturates)
34g carbohydrate
0.2g salt

125g (4oz) unsalted butter, very soft
125g (4oz) caster sugar
grated zest of 1 lemon
2 medium eggs, beaten
125g (4oz) self-raising flour, sifted

For the icing and decoration
175g (6oz) icing sugar
black and assorted writing icings
jelly diamonds and Smarties
black liquorice laces, cut into short
lengths

1 Preheat the oven to 190°C (170°C fan oven) mark 5. Line a 12-hole bun tin with paper cases.

2 Put the butter, caster sugar and lemon zest into a mixing bowl and, using a hand-held electric whisk, beat until light and fluffy. Add the eggs, a little at a time, beating well after each addition. Fold in the flour. Divide the mixture between the paper cases. Bake for 20 minutes or until golden and risen. Transfer to a wire rack to cool completely.

3 For the icing, sift the icing sugar into a bowl. Stir in 1–2 tbsp warm water, a few drops at a time, until you have a smooth, spreadable icing. If necessary, slice the tops off the cooled cakes to make them level. Cover the top of each cake with icing.

4 Decorate the cakes to make kittens' faces. Use black writing icing for the eyes, halve the jelly diamonds for the ears, press a Smartie in the centre for a nose, and use black writing icing to draw on a mouth. Use different coloured writing icing for the pupils and markings. Press on liquorice whiskers.

Red Nose Buns

Makes 36
Preparation Time
20 minutes
Cooking Time
12–15 minutes,
plus cooling
and setting

Per Bun
39 calories
1g fat
(of which 1g saturates)
7g carbohydrate
0g salt

50g (2oz) unsalted butter, very soft
50g (2oz) caster sugar
1 medium egg, beaten
50g (2oz) self-raising flour
¼ tsp baking powder
1 ripe banana, peeled and mashed

For the icing and decoration
125g (4oz) icing sugar, sifted
about 1 tbsp orange juice
red glacé cherries or round red jelly sweets

1 Preheat the oven to 190°C (170°C fan oven) mark 5. Arrange about 36 petits fours cases on baking sheets.

2 Put the butter, caster sugar, egg, flour and baking powder into a food processor and whiz until smooth and well mixed. Add the banana and whiz for 1 minute. Put a teaspoonful of the mixture into each paper case.

3 Bake for 12–15 minutes until golden. Transfer to a wire rack to cool completely.

4 For the icing, mix the icing sugar with the orange juice until smooth and just thick enough to coat the back of a spoon. Top each bun with a small blob of icing and stick half a glacé cherry or a jelly sweet on each one. Stand the cakes upright on the wire rack and leave for about 1 hour to set.

Star Cupcakes

Makes 12	125g (4oz) butter, softened
Preparation Time	125g (4oz) caster sugar
40 minutes,	2 large eggs
plus drying	grated zest and juice of 1 large unwaxed lemon
Cooking Time	125g (4oz) self-raising flour
20 minutes,	1 tsp baking powder
plus cooling	
	For the icing and decoration
Per Cupcake	1 × quantity fondant icing (see below)
226 calories	cornflour to dust
10g fat	125g (4oz) sugarpaste
(of which 6g saturates)	edible glue
34g carbohydrate	edible glitter in silver and gold
0.4g salt	star-shaped cutter
	paintbrush

1 Preheat the oven to 180°C (160°C fan oven) mark 3. Line a 12-hole muffin tin with paper muffin cases.

2 Put the butter and sugar in a large bowl and beat with a hand-held whisk until light and fluffy. Beat the eggs in a separate bowl, then gradually add them to the butter and sugar mixture, beating well between each addition. Add the lemon zest and beat well.

3 Sift in the flour and baking powder, and fold in with a large metal spoon. If the mixture needs loosening a bit, add a little lemon juice. The mixture should gently drop off a spoon. Divide the mixture equally between the paper cases and bake for 20 minutes or until firm to the touch and golden. Transfer to a wire rack to cool completely.

4 For the icing, make the fondant icing, ice the cupcakes and leave to dry.

5 Dust a work surface with cornflour, and roll out the sugarpaste until it is about 3mm (¹/₈in) thick. Cut out 12 star shapes using a star-shaped cutter.

6 Paint edible glue over each star, making sure they are completely covered, before dipping 6 stars in gold glitter and 6 in silver glitter. Dab a tiny bit of edible glue on the centre of each cupcake and carefully place a star on top.

Fondant icing

225g (8oz) fondant sugar

Make up the fondant icing following the instructions on the packet.

Jewelled Cupcakes

Makes 12
Preparation Time
40 minutes
Cooking Time
30 minutes,
plus cooling
and setting

Per Cupcake
276 calories
10g fat
(of which 4g saturates)
46g carbohydrate
0.4g salt

75g (3oz) unsalted butter, softened
150g (5oz) caster sugar
3 medium eggs
175g (6oz) self-raising flour, sifted
175g (6oz) mincemeat

For the decoration
75g (3oz) apricot glaze (see below)
50g (2oz) toasted flaked almonds
50g (2oz) ready-to-eat apricots, chopped
12 glacé cherries
40g (1½oz) caster sugar
1 tbsp unsalted butter

1 Preheat the oven to 190°C (170°C fan oven) mark 5. Line a 12-hole muffin tin with paper muffin cases.

2 Using a hand-held electric whisk, whisk the butter and sugar in a bowl, or beat with a wooden spoon, until pale and creamy. Gradually whisk in the eggs until just combined. Using a metal spoon, fold in the flour and mincemeat until combined. Divide the mixture equally between the paper cases.

3 Bake for 20 minutes or until golden and risen. Leave to cool in the tin for 5 minutes, then transfer to a wire rack to cool completely.

4 For the decoration, brush each cake with a little apricot glaze, then scatter on a few almonds and apricots and a cherry. Stand the cakes upright on the wire rack.

5 Put the sugar and 1 tbsp cold water into a small pan and gently heat until the sugar dissolves. Increase the heat and bubble for 3–4 minutes until the sugar caramelises and turns golden in colour. Remove from the heat and quickly stir in the butter until combined. Being very careful, drizzle the hot caramel over the top of each cake. Leave for about 10 minutes to set.

Apricot Glaze

450g (1lb) apricot jam
2 tbsp water

Put the jam and water into a pan, heat gently, stirring occasionally until melted. Boil the jam rapidly for 1 minute, then strain through a fine sieve – pushing as much mixture through as possible. Pour the glaze into a clean, sterilised jar. Seal with a clean lid and cool. It can be chilled for up to two months. To use, brush over cakes before applying almond paste, or use to glaze fruit finishes. If the consistency is a little stiff, then stir in a few drops of boiled water.

Sea Breeze Cupcakes

Makes 12
Preparation Time
40 minutes
Cooking Time
20 minutes,
plus cooling
and setting

Per Cupcake
287 calories
6g fat
(of which 4g saturates)
61g carbohydrate
0.1g salt

1 pink grapefruit (about 350g/12oz)
50g (2oz) ready-to-eat dried cranberries
250g (9oz) self-raising flour, sifted
125g (4oz) caster sugar
50ml (2fl oz) milk
1 medium egg, beaten
75g (3oz) unsalted butter, melted
1 tsp baking powder

For the icing and decoration
300g (11oz) fondant icing sugar, sifted
red and yellow food colouring
50g (2oz) apricot glaze (see page 72)
edible silver balls
cocktail umbrellas (optional)

1 Preheat the oven to 190°C (170°C fan oven) mark 5. Line a 12-hole muffin tin with paper muffin cases.

2 Grate the zest from half the grapefruit into a bowl. Set aside. Cut the top and bottom off the grapefruit and stand it upright on a board. Using a serrated knife, cut away the pith in a downward motion. Cut in between the membranes to remove the segments. Whiz the segments in a food processor until puréed.

3 Transfer the purée into the bowl with the zest. Add the cranberries, flour, caster sugar, milk, egg, melted butter and baking powder and stir with a spatula until just combined. Divide the mixture equally between the paper cases.

4 Bake for 20 minutes or until golden and risen. Leave to cool in the tin for 5 minutes, then transfer to a wire rack to cool completely.

5 For the icing, put the icing sugar into a bowl and add enough water (2–4 tbsp) to make a smooth icing. Add a few drops of food colouring to make it pinky-orange in colour. Brush the tops of the cakes with the apricot glaze, then spoon a little icing on to each cake to flood the top. Decorate with the silver balls. Stand the cakes upright on the wire rack and leave for about 1 hour to set. Decorate with a cocktail umbrella once set, if you like.

Truffle Kisses Cupcakes

Makes 18	150g (5oz) unsalted butter, softened
Preparation Time	200g (7oz) caster sugar
40 minutes	3 medium eggs
Cooking Time	75g (3oz) self-raising flour, sifted
30 minutes,	200g (7oz) plain flour, sifted
plus cooling	½ tsp bicarbonate of soda
and setting	75g (3oz) roasted chopped hazelnuts
	200ml (7fl oz) buttermilk
Per Cupcake	15g (½oz) dark chocolate, finely grated
317 calories	
20g fat	**For the topping and decoration**
(of which 10g saturates)	200ml (7fl oz) double cream
34g carbohydrate	150g (5oz) dark chocolate
0.2g salt	100g (3½oz) milk chocolate, finely chopped
	18 small chocolate truffles (optional)

1 Preheat the oven to 180°C (160°C fan oven) mark 4. Line a 12-hole and a 6-hole muffin tin with paper muffin cases.

2 Using a hand-held electric whisk, whisk the butter and sugar in a bowl, or beat with a wooden spoon, until pale and creamy. Gradually whisk in the eggs until just combined. Using a metal spoon, fold in both flours, the bicarbonate of soda, hazelnuts, buttermilk and grated chocolate until combined. Divide the mixture equally between the paper cases.

3 Bake for 20–25 minutes until golden and risen. Leave to cool in the tin for 5 minutes, then transfer to a wire rack to cool completely.

4 For the topping, heat the cream in a small saucepan until nearly boiling. Finely chop 100g (3½oz) dark chocolate and put into a bowl along with all the milk chocolate. Pour the hot cream over the chocolate and leave to stand for 5 minutes, then stir gently until smooth. Chill the mixture for 15–20 minutes until thickened slightly.

5 Using a palette knife, spread a little chocolate cream over the top of each cake. Finely grate the remaining dark chocolate over the top of each cake. Finish each with a chocolate truffle, if you like. Stand the cakes upright on the wire rack and leave for about 1 hour to set.

Secret Garden Cupcakes

Makes 12
Preparation Time
45 minutes
Cooking Time
40 minutes,
plus cooling

Per Cupcake
398 calories
20g fat
(of which 13g saturates)
53g carbohydrate
0.5g salt

200g (7oz) fresh strawberries,
hulled and halved
200g (7oz) caster sugar
150g (5oz) unsalted butter, softened
3 medium eggs
200g (7oz) self-raising flour, sifted
½ tsp bicarbonate of soda
50ml (2fl oz) buttermilk

For the topping and decoration
125g (4oz) unsalted butter, softened
250g (9oz) icing sugar, sifted
green food colouring
ladybird, bumble bee and butterfly
sugar decorations (optional)

1 Preheat the oven to 190°C (170°C fan oven) mark 5. Line a 12-hole muffin tin with paper muffin cases.

2 Put the strawberries and 50g (2oz) caster sugar into a heatproof bowl and cover with clingfilm. Put over a pan of barely simmering water and cook gently for 30 minutes.

3 Meanwhile, using a hand-held electric whisk, whisk the butter and remaining caster sugar in a bowl, or beat with a wooden spoon, until pale and creamy. Gradually whisk in the eggs until just combined. Using a metal spoon, fold in the flour, bicarbonate of soda and buttermilk until combined. Divide the mixture equally between the paper cases.

4 Bake for 20 minutes or until golden and risen. Leave to cool in the tin for 5 minutes. Meanwhile, pass the strawberries and juice through a sieve into a shallow bowl. Discard the strawberries.

5 Using a cocktail stick, prick the top of the cakes all over. Dip the top of each cake into the strawberry syrup, then transfer to a wire rack to cool completely.

6 For the topping, put the butter into a bowl and whisk until fluffy. Gradually whisk in half the icing sugar, then add 1 tbsp boiling water, a little green food colouring and the remaining icing sugar and whisk until light and fluffy.

7 Insert a star nozzle into a piping bag, then fill the bag with the buttercream and pipe in a zigzag pattern on top of each cake. Decorate with the sugar ladybirds, butterflies and bumble bees, if you like.

Pretty Pink Cupcakes

Makes 12
Preparation Time
35 minutes
Cooking Time
20 minutes,
plus cooling

Per Cupcake
361 calories
14g fat
(of which 6g saturates)
58g carbohydrate
0.2g salt

150g (5oz) raw beetroot, peeled and finely grated
200g (7oz) self-raising flour, sifted
½ tsp bicarbonate of soda
150g (5oz) caster sugar
zest 1 orange
2 medium eggs
100ml (3½fl oz) sunflower oil
125ml (4fl oz) buttermilk

For the topping and decoration
100g (3½oz) unsalted butter, softened
350g (12oz) icing sugar, sifted
50ml (2fl oz) milk
pink food colouring
ready-made pink or red sugar flowers (optional)

1 Preheat the oven to 190°C (170°C fan oven) mark 5. Line a 12-hole muffin tin with paper muffin cases.

2 Put the beetroot, flour, bicarbonate of soda, caster sugar and orange zest into a bowl. Put the eggs, oil and buttermilk into a jug and lightly beat together until combined. Pour the egg mixture into the flour and stir with a spatula until just combined. Divide the mixture equally between the paper cases.

3 Bake for 20 minutes or until lightly golden and risen. Leave to cool in the tin for 5 minutes, then transfer to a wire rack to cool completely.

4 For the topping, put the butter into a bowl and whisk until fluffy. Gradually whisk in half the icing sugar, then add the milk, a little pink food colouring and the remaining icing sugar and whisk until light and fluffy.

5 Insert a star nozzle into a piping bag, then fill the bag with the buttercream and pipe small swirls all the way around the top of each cake. Decorate with the sugar flowers, if using.

Rosy Cupcakes

Makes 12
Preparation Time
15 minutes
Cooking Time
20 minutes,
plus cooling
and setting

Per Cupcake
233 calories
10g fat
(of which 2g saturates)
36g carbohydrate
0.4g salt

125g (4oz) self-raising flour, sifted
125g (4oz) caster sugar, sifted
125g (4oz) soft margarine or butter
1 tsp baking powder
2 large eggs
1 tsp pure vanilla extract

For the icing and decoration
200g (7oz) icing sugar, sifted
gel food colouring
12 sugar roses

1 Preheat the oven to 180°C (160°C fan oven) mark 3. Line a 12-hole muffin tin with paper muffin cases.

2 Put the flour, sugar, baking powder, margarine, eggs and vanilla in a mixer and beat until the mixture is pale and creamy.

3 Divide heaped teaspoons of the mixture into the paper cases and bake for 20 minutes or until golden, and firm and springy to the touch. Transfer the cakes to a wire rack to cool completely.

4 For the icing, put the icing sugar in a bowl and slowly add enough boiling water until you have a thick soup consistency. Add the food colouring and pour over the cupcakes. Leave for about 10 minutes before carefully placing a rose on top of each cupcake.

Cook's Tip
Sugar roses are made from flower paste and can be bought from sugarcraft shops. They are also readily available from on-line sugarcraft shops in a variety of colours and sizes.

Valentine Cupcakes

Makes 10
Preparation Time
30 minutes
Cooking Time
20 minutes,
plus cooling

125g (4oz) self-raising flour
125g (4oz) caster sugar
1 tsp baking powder
125g (4oz) soft margarine or butter
2 large eggs
1 tsp pure vanilla extract

Per Cupcake
291 calories
12g fat
(of which 3g saturates)
46g carbohydrate
0.5g salt

For the icing and decoration
1 × quantity plain glacé icing (see below)
food colouring of your choice (preferably gel)
edible glue
red edible glitter
metallic foil cupcake cases

1 Preheat the oven to 190°C (170° fan oven) mark 5. Carefully oil a 12-hole straight-sided silicone heart-shaped muffin tray.

2 Sift the flour, sugar and baking powder into a bowl, food processor or mixer. Add the margarine, eggs and vanilla and beat until pale and creamy. Spoon the mixture carefully into the muffin tray, place on a metal baking sheet and bake for 20 minutes or until golden and firm to the touch. Leave to cool in the muffin tray, then turn the cupcakes out on to a wire rack and leave to cool completely.

3 To create a level surface, slice the tops off the cupcakes and turn the cakes upside down (you will be icing the bottom of the cakes). Make the glacé icing and tint it to your chosen colour. Drizzle the icing all over the cakes and let it run down the sides.

4 Before the icing is completely dry, lay out all your metallic cupcake cases. Dip your fingers into a bowl of cold water, then lift the cakes onto the cases (this stops the icing sticking to your fingers). Carefully mould the cases around the hearts.

5 When the icing is completely dry, paint the entire top with edible glue and dip into the glitter.

Glacé icing

225g (8oz) icing sugar, sifted
juice of 1 large lemon or 2 tbsp boiling water
gel food colouring of your choice

Put the sifted icing sugar in a bowl and add the liquid slowly, a little at a time. Stir until smooth (stop adding the liquid once the icing is a smooth, spreadable consistency).

Mother's Day Cupcakes

Makes 20
Preparation Time
20 minutes
Cooking Time
10-12 minutes,
plus cooling
and setting

Per cake:
107 calories
5g fat
(of which 3g saturates)
16g carbohydrate
(12g total sugars)

100g (3½oz) unsalted butter,
softened
100g (3½oz) caster sugar
100y (3½oz) self-raising flour
2 medium eggs

For the icing and decoration
125g (4oz) icing sugar, sifted
pink and green food colouring
hundreds and thousands

1 Preheat the oven to 200°C (180°C fan) mark 6. Put 20 mini paper muffin or cupcake cases into holes of a mini muffin or cupcake tin. If you don't have one, put the cases (two cases thick) directly on a baking sheet.

2 Put the butter, sugar, flour and eggs into a large bowl and beat with a wooden spoon until mixed. Divide the mixture equally between the paper cases.

3 Bake for 10-12 minutes or until golden and a skewer inserted into centre comes out clean. Transfer the cakes (still in their cases) to a wire rack to cool completely.

4 Divide the sifted icing sugar between two bowls. If using liquid food colouring, add a little pink to one bowl and green to the other, then stir to check the consistency. To each bowl, add just enough water to bring mixture together to a smooth, spoonable consistency. If using colouring pastes, dye white icings, already at the right consistency, by dipping the end of a cocktail stick into dyes, then into the icing. Stir to mix.

5 Cover top of each cake with green or pink icing. Sprinkle over hundreds and thousands. Serve or leave to set first.

Easter Cupcakes

Makes 6	2 medium eggs
Preparation Time	75g (3oz) caster sugar
30 minutes	150ml (¼ pint) sunflower oil
Cooking Time	150g (5oz) plain flour, sifted
30 minutes,	½ tsp baking powder
plus cooling	1 tsp vanilla extract
and setting	15g (½oz) Rice Krispies
Per Cupcake	**For the topping and decoration**
378 calories	100g (3½oz) white chocolate,
27g fat	broken into pieces
(of which 8g saturates)	15g (½oz) unsalted butter
32g carbohydrate	25g (1oz) Rice Krispies
0.2g salt	12 chocolate mini eggs

1 Preheat the oven to 180°C (160°C fan oven) mark 4. Line a 6-hole muffin tin with paper muffin cases.

2 Separate the eggs, putting the whites in a clean, grease-free bowl and the egg yolks in another. Add the sugar to the yolks and whisk with a hand-held electric whisk until pale and creamy. Then whisk in the oil until combined.

3 Whisk the egg whites until soft peaks form. Using a metal spoon, quickly fold the flour, baking powder, vanilla extract and Rice Krispies into the egg yolk mixture until just combined. Add half the egg whites to the egg yolk mixture to loosen, then carefully fold in the remaining egg whites. Divide the mixture equally between the paper cases.

4 Bake for 20–25 minutes until golden and risen. Leave to cool in the tin for 5 minutes, then transfer to a wire rack to cool completely.

5 For the topping, put the chocolate and butter into a heatproof bowl and place over a pan of barely simmering water, making sure the base of the bowl doesn't touch the water. Gently heat until the chocolate has melted, stirring occasionally until smooth. Remove the bowl from the heat, add the Rice Krispies and fold through until coated. Spoon the mixture on top of each cake, pressing down lightly, then top each with 2 chocolate eggs. Stand the cakes upright on the wire rack and leave for about 1 hour to set.

Halloween Cupcakes

Makes 12
Preparation Time
30 minutes,
plus drying
Cooking Time
20 minutes,
plus cooling

Per Cupcake
257 calories
10g fat
(of which 2g saturates)
42g carbohydrate
0.4g salt

1 × quantity lemon cupcake mixture
(see Citrus Cupcakes, page 27)

For the icing and decoration
1 × quantity glacé icing (see Valentine Cupcakes,
page 83)
black and orange food colouring paste
100g (3½oz) each black and white sugarpaste
edible glue
small paintbrush

1 Make the cupcakes as per the method described. Leave to cool completely before decorating.

2 For the icing, make up the glacé icing and divide into two portions; use the food colouring to make one black and the other deep orange. Divide the cupcakes into two batches, and ice one batch black and the other batch orange. Leave them to dry completely.

3 Divide the white sugarpaste into 6 and make a ghost from each piece by flattening out into the shape of a ghost. Use edible glue to stick it on to a black-iced cupcake. Let the ghost trail over the edge of the cake. Take some tiny bits of black sugarpaste, and stick them on to make a ghoulish face for the ghost.

4 Make the spider using a bit of black sugarpaste the size of a broad bean, and stick it onto an orange-iced cake using edible glue. Make 8 legs out of slivers of black paste, and stick them on the top. Add a strip of black for the web and create a face and fangs out of white sugarpaste. For the eyes, take 2 elongated egg shapes of white sugarpaste, add black pupils and stick onto an orange-iced cake.

Bonfire Night Cupcakes

Makes about 12

Preparation Time
30 minutes

Cooking Time
20 minutes,
plus cooling
and setting

Per Cupcake
254 calories
10g fat
(of which 2g saturates)
42g carbohydrate
0.4g salt

1 × quantity lemon cupcake mixture
(see Citrus Cupcakes, page 27)

For the icing and decoration
1 × quantity glacé icing (see Valentine Cupcakes,
page 83)
gel food colourings
2 tbsp royal icing (see below)
dragees (multicoloured if possible)
edible glitter (optional)
3–4 piping bags with fine nozzles

1 Make the cupcakes as per the method described.
Leave to cool completely before decorating.

2 For the icing, make up the glacé icing and add deep
navy blue to imitate the night sky. Allow the icing to
dry completely.

3 Separate the royal icing into as many bowls as you
want colours, and tint them accordingly with the food
colouring. Using piping bags with fine nozzles, pipe on
whatever firework you like such as Catherine wheels,
rockets and shooting stars.

4 Sprinkle a tiny bit of edible glitter over them if you
want, and add the dragees, which may need a tiny
dab of royal icing underneath them to hold them in place.

Royal icing

1 large egg white
250g (9oz) icing sugar, sifted
1 tsp freshly squeezed lemon juice

Put all the ingredients into a bowl, and stir until the
mixture is smooth and stands in stiff peaks. If the
mixture is too stiff, add a few drops of lemon juice or
boiling water. If it is too runny, add a little more sifted
icing sugar. The icing can be made in advance and stored
in the fridge for up to 3 days. Cover with clingfilm and
store in an airtight container.

Christmas Day Cupcakes

Makes about 12
Preparation Time
20 minutes
Cooking Time
20 minutes,
plus cooling
and setting

Per Cupcake
268 calories
10g fat
(of which 6g saturates)
45g carbohydrate
0.4g salt

50g (2oz) raisins
2 tbsp rum or brandy
125g (4oz) glacé cherries
125g (4oz) butter, softened
125g (4oz) golden caster sugar
2 large eggs
125g (4oz) self-raising flour
1 tsp baking powder
½ tsp mixed spice
for 1 hour, drained

For the icing and decoration
1 × quantity fondant icing (see Star Cupcakes, page 71)
2 tbsp royal icing (see Bonfire Night Cupcakes, page 91)
silver dragees
piping bag fitted with a fine nozzle

1 Put the raisins and brandy or rum into a small bowl and set aside for 1 hour. Preheat the oven to 180°C (160°C fan oven) mark 3. Line a 12-hole muffin tin with paper muffin cases. Rinse the glacé cherries, pat dry and then roughly chop.

2 Put the butter and sugar in a bowl and beat together until light and fluffy. Beat the eggs in a separate bowl with a hand-held electric whisk, and gradually add to the butter and sugar mixture, beating well between each addition. Add the contents of the bowl containing the soaked raisins, and beat well.

3 Sift the flour, baking powder and mixed spice on to a large plate, and toss the chopped cherries into the flour. Carefully add to the wet mixture, and fold in with a large metal spoon. Spoon carefully into the paper cases and bake for 20 minutes until golden and firm to the touch. Transfer to a wire rack to cool completely.

4 For the icing, make up the fondant icing and use to ice the cupcakes. Leave to set.

5 Put the royal icing into a piping bag, and pipe Christmas tree shapes on to the cakes. Add silver dragees to the trees as decorations.

Wedding Cupcakes

Make 12

Preparation Time
30 minutes

Cooking time
15 minutes, plus
cooling and
setting

Per cupcake
375 cals
20g fat
(of which 12g saturates)
50g carbohydrate
0.6g salt

1 × quantity cupcake mixture
(see Fairy Cakes, page 64)
12 pink paper cupcake cases

For the icing and decoration
pink food colouring paste
500g (1lb 2oz) buttercream
(see page 65)
12 rose-themed cupcake surrounds

1 Make the cupcakes in the paper cases as per the method described. Leave to cool completely before decorating.

2 For the icing, dip the tip of a cocktail stick into the desired shade of pink food colouring, then dip into the buttercream. Use a spatula to start mixing in the colour, stopping when the buttercream is marbled.

3 Fit a piping bag with a 1cm (½in) open-star nozzle and fill with the buttercream. Hold the piping bag just above the centre of a cupcake and start piping with even pressure. Swirl the icing in a spiral from the centre towards the edges, making sure the entire surface of the cake is covered. By starting in the centre (rather than the outside edge as is normal) you should create a rose effect. Repeat with the remaining cupcakes. Leave to set for at least 1 hour.

4 Fit the surrounds around the cupcakes.

Cook's Tips

It is best to decorate these cupcakes on the day that they're needed, but the undecorated cakes can be made and frozen ahead. Bake, cool and freeze the cupcakes up to one month before the event. When needed, allow the cakes to thaw at room temperature before decorating. For added wow-factor, roll out coloured sugarpaste (ideally mixed with gum tragacanth, a natural gum you can get from specialist cake shops or via websites) until 5mm (¼in) thick, then stamp out small heart shapes. You could even pipe the initials of the bride and groom on to the hearts. Stick the hearts (standing upright) into the top edge of each iced cupcake.

Index

KITCHEN NOTES

Both metric and imperial measures are given for the recipes. Follow either set of measures, not a mixture of both, as they are not interchangeable.

All spoon measures are level.
1 tsp = 5ml spoon; 1 tbsp = 15ml spoon.

Ovens and grills must be preheated to the specified temperature.

Medium eggs should be used except where otherwise specified. Free-range eggs are recommended.

Note that some recipes contain raw or lightly cooked eggs. The young, elderly, pregnant women and anyone with an immune-deficiency disease should avoid these because of the slight risk of salmonella.

Photographers: Steve Baxter (pages 24, 25, 84 and 85); Nicki Dowey (pages 21, 23, 34, 60, 63, 65, 68 and 69); Brian Hatton (pages 28 and 29); William Lingwood (pages 12, 13, 26, 27, 48, 49, 58, 59, 66, 67, 70, 71, 80, 81, 82, 83, 88, 89, 90, 91, 92, 93 and 94); Craig Robertson (page 22); Lucinda Symons (pages 5, 6, 7, 8, 9, 10, 11, 14, 15, 16, 17, 18, 19, 20, 30, 31, 32, 33, 35, 36, 37, 38, 39, 42, 43, 44, 45, 46, 47, 50, 51, 52, 53, 54, 55, 56, 57, 61, 62, 64, 72, 73, 74, 75, 76, 77, 78, 79, 86 and 87); Kate Whitaker (pages 40 and 41)

Home Economists: Joanna Farrow, Emma Jane Frost, Teresa Goldfinch, Alice Hart, Lucy McKelvie, Kim Morphew, Bridget Sargeson and Mari Mererid Williams

Stylists: Tamzin Ferdinando, Wei Tang, Helen Trent and Fanny Ward

First published in Great Britain in 2012
by Collins & Brown
10 Southcombe Street
London W14 0RA

An imprint of Anova Books Company Ltd

The Good Housekeeping website is
www.allaboutyou.com/goodhousekeeping

ISBN 978-1-908449-28-3

A catalogue record for this book is available from the British Library.

Reproduction by Dot Gradations Ltd, UK
Printed and bound by 1010 Printing International Ltd, China

This book can be ordered direct from the publisher. Contact the marketing department, but try your bookshop first.

www.anovabooks.com